PAPER AIRPLANES TO MAKE AND FLY

JIM RAZZI

SCHOLASTIC INC.
New York Toronto London Auckland Sydney

To Wendy

— J. R.

ISBN 0-590-42050-X

12 11 10 9 8 7 6 5 4   0 1 2 3 4 5/9

Printed in the U.S.A.   08
First Scholastic printing, April 1990

CONTENTS

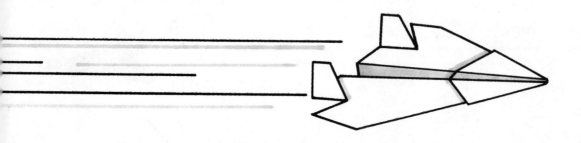

INTRODUCTION

The models in this book are easy to make and fun to fly if you follow the simple step-by-step instructions.

Here are some helpful hints:
1. Go step by step! Read each instruction. Look at each drawing. You may find it easier if you read through all the instructions for a model before you begin.
2. It is very important to hold your model in the same direction as the illustrations.
3. Follow the arrows in the illustrations when making folds.
4. Carefully line things up. Fold precisely. Press folds firmly.

Once you know how to make the models, experiment. Use a model as a base and create your own new design.

One more thought before you solo. If you fly indoors, make sure you don't crash-land into the dog, the cat, or anything that is fragile!

HAPPY LANDINGS!

YOU'LL NEED:

Tape
A pencil
Scissors
Paper clips
A ruler
8½″ × 11″ paper

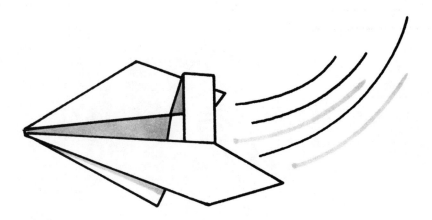

WHAT KIND OF PAPER TO USE:

Heavyweight typewriting paper, computer paper, and copier paper are good choices for making these models. All of these papers are available in stationery stores. For certain models, one type of paper might work better than another. If a plane doesn't seem to fly well when made with one type or weight of paper, try making it with a different type or weight.

Computer paper is sold in a "form-feed" package. This means that the sheets are connected. Simply tear off each sheet as needed. Remove the strips with the holes from the sides, and you will have a standard sheet of paper.

Remember that very lightweight paper such as loose-leaf notepaper or onionskin is too thin to use for the models and will *not* work well.

TIPS ON FLYING YOUR MODELS:

If you are flying your models outside, a calm day is best for flying because paper is so easily affected by the wind. Keep in mind that a model that flies beautifully indoors might need extra weight on its nose outdoors. Experiment with paper clips.

Some models will also need a little adjustment on the control elevators for a smoother flight. A control elevator is the back edge or tip of a wing.

The two main flight problems are stalls and nosedives.

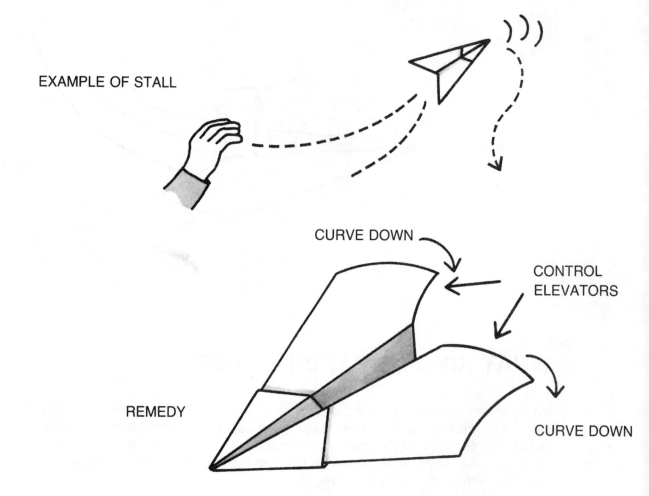

EXAMPLE OF STALL

CURVE DOWN

CONTROL
ELEVATORS

REMEDY

CURVE DOWN

If your model stalls (the nose goes up as you launch it), curve down the control elevators. This will force the nose down. If the nose of your model dives as soon as you launch it, curve the control elevators up. This will force the nose up.

It's easy to remember. When you want the nose to go up, curve the control elevators up. When you want the nose to go down, curve the control elevators down. You will have to experiment to find out how much to curve the control elevators. Always make sure that both control elevators curve to the same degree.

EXAMPLE OF NOSEDIVE

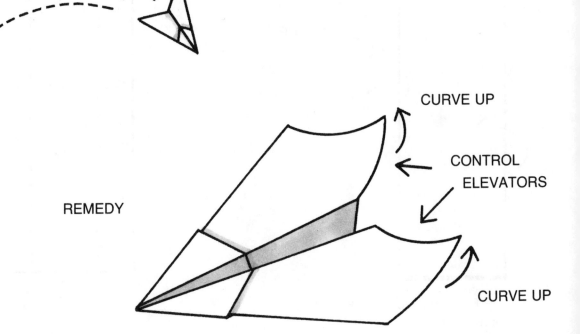

CURVE UP

CONTROL
ELEVATORS

REMEDY

CURVE UP

TO LAUNCH:

Launching a paper airplane just takes a little practice. To launch a model indoors, use a quick, smooth "pushing" motion instead of a "throwing" motion.

Each model reacts differently outdoors, but usually you can launch your plane with more force than you need indoors. It helps to use a snap of the wrist to begin a successful outdoor flight.

THE FOUR-STEP FOLD

You will use the Four-Step Fold to begin most of the models in this book. Whenever you are told to do the Four-Step Fold, be sure that your paper looks like step 4 before you continue making your model.

Either practice and memorize the fold or refer to this page when you need to make the Four-Step Fold.

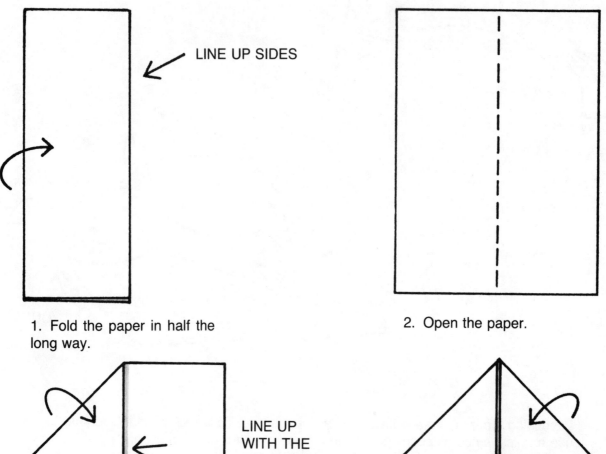

LINE UP SIDES

1. Fold the paper in half the long way.

2. Open the paper.

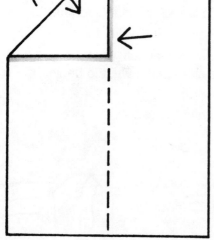

LINE UP WITH THE FOLD LINE

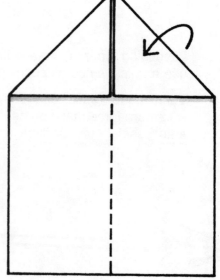

3. Fold the top corner so that the top edge meets the fold line.

4. Fold the other top corner so that the top edge meets the fold line.

RAINY DAY FLYER

If it's a rainy day and you're in a hurry to fly, here's a gentle flyer that will float across a room.

Take a piece of paper and do the Four-Step Fold. If necessary look at page 8 for instructions. Your paper should look like step 4 of the Four-Step Fold before you continue.

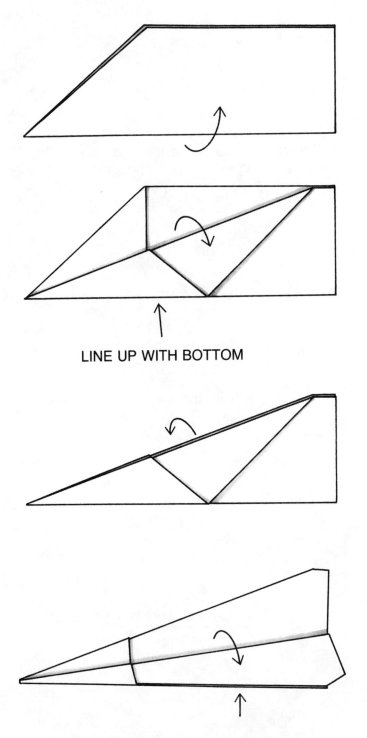

LINE UP WITH BOTTOM

LINE UP FIRST WING WITH BOTTOM

1. Refold the paper in half with the folded corners inside.

2. Fold the first side, lining up the slanted edge with the bottom.

3. Now do the same thing with the other side. Make sure that both sides have been folded evenly and line up with the bottom.

4. Fold the first wing, lining it up with the bottom.

CONTINUED ▷

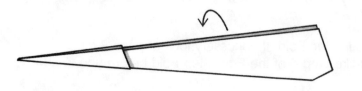

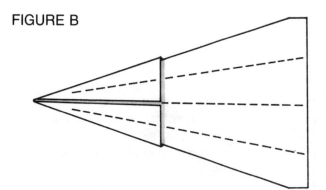

5. Fold the second wing, lining it up with the first.

FIGURE A

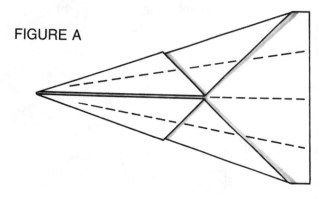

6. Open the paper as shown in figure A. Lay the paper flat.

FIGURE B

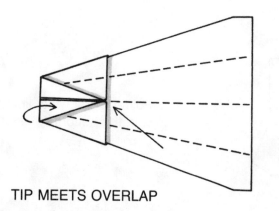

7. Turn the paper over as shown in figure B.

8. Fold the tip so that it meets the overlap.

TIP MEETS OVERLAP

CONTINUED ▷

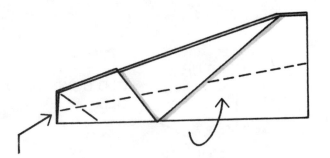

FOLDED TIP IS INSIDE

9. Refold the paper in half with the folded tip inside.

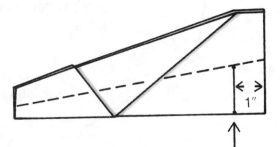

DRAW LINE UP
TO WING FOLD

10. With your ruler, measure a line one inch from the back edge. Draw the line up to the wing as shown.

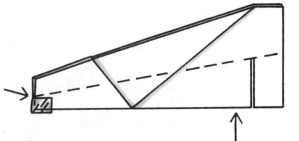

TAPE NOSE
BELOW FOLD   CUT UP TO WING FOLD

11. Then cut through *both* sides of the paper along the line you've drawn. Don't cut above the wing fold. Tape the nose together in front *below* the fold.

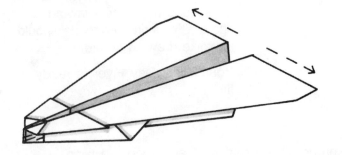

12. Open the model and level the wings.

CONTINUED ▷

RAINY DAY FLYER

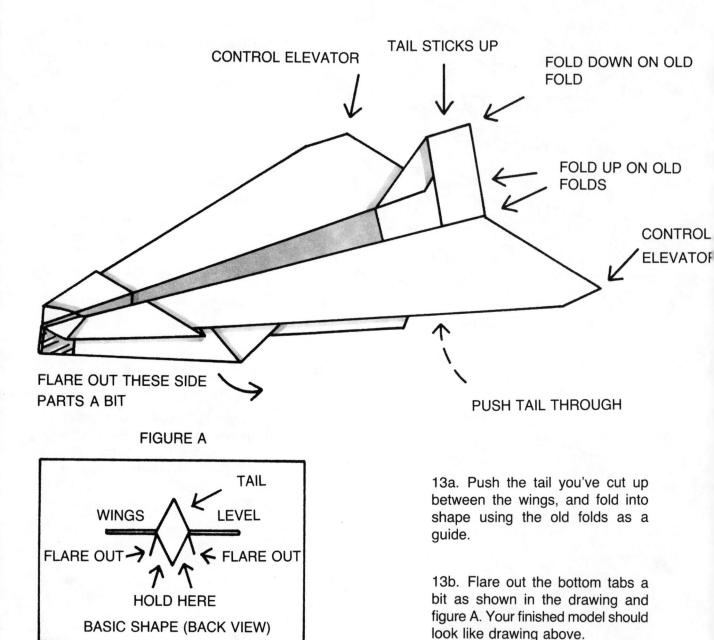

CONTROL ELEVATOR

TAIL STICKS UP

FOLD DOWN ON OLD FOLD

FOLD UP ON OLD FOLDS

CONTROL ELEVATOR

FLARE OUT THESE SIDE PARTS A BIT

PUSH TAIL THROUGH

FIGURE A

TAIL

WINGS   LEVEL

FLARE OUT →   ← FLARE OUT

HOLD HERE

BASIC SHAPE (BACK VIEW)

13a. Push the tail you've cut up between the wings, and fold into shape using the old folds as a guide.

13b. Flare out the bottom tabs a bit as shown in the drawing and figure A. Your finished model should look like drawing above.

Your Rainy Day Flyer is ready to fly.

FLYING NOTES:

It's important that the tail is folded properly and doesn't lean. Keep the wings level and hold the plane by only the bottom fold so that the bottom tabs will stay flared. (See figure A.) Your plane will float gently through the air and glide to a smooth landing.

Named for its V-shaped body, this is a very stable flyer. Make the V-Glider with heavyweight typewriting paper or another heavyweight paper.

Take a piece of paper and do the Four-Step Fold. If necessary turn to page 8 for instructions. Your paper should look like step 4 of the Four-Step Fold before you continue.

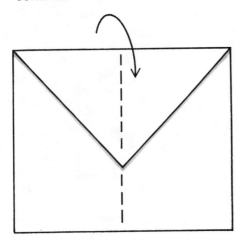

1. Carefully fold the triangle as shown, so that the tip of the triangle rests on the fold line.

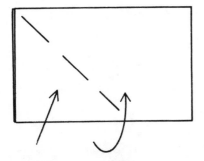

:OLDED PART IS INSIDE

2. Refold the paper in half with the folded tip inside.

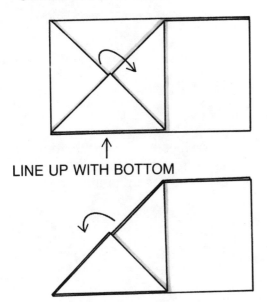

LINE UP WITH BOTTOM

3. Fold the first corner, lining up the side edge with the bottom.

4. Fold the second corner the same way.

CONTINUED ▷

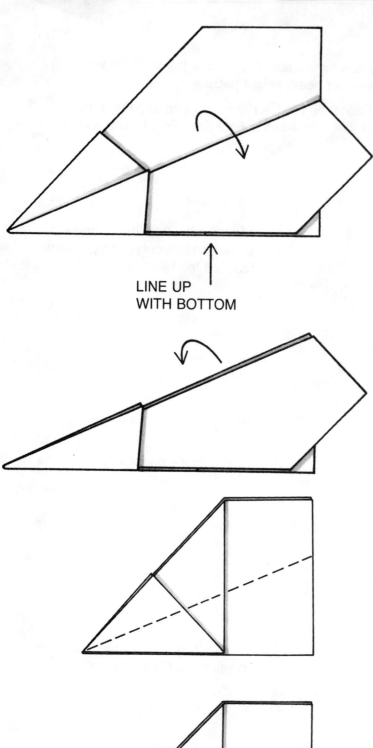

LINE UP
WITH BOTTOM

5. Fold the first wing, lining it up with the bottom.

6. Fold the second wing, lining it up with the first.

7. Open the two folds you just made and lay the paper flat.

8. With your ruler, measure a line 1 inch from the back edge as shown. Draw the line up to the wing.

←1"→

DRAW LINE UP TO
THE WING FOLD

CONTINUED ▷

V-GLIDER

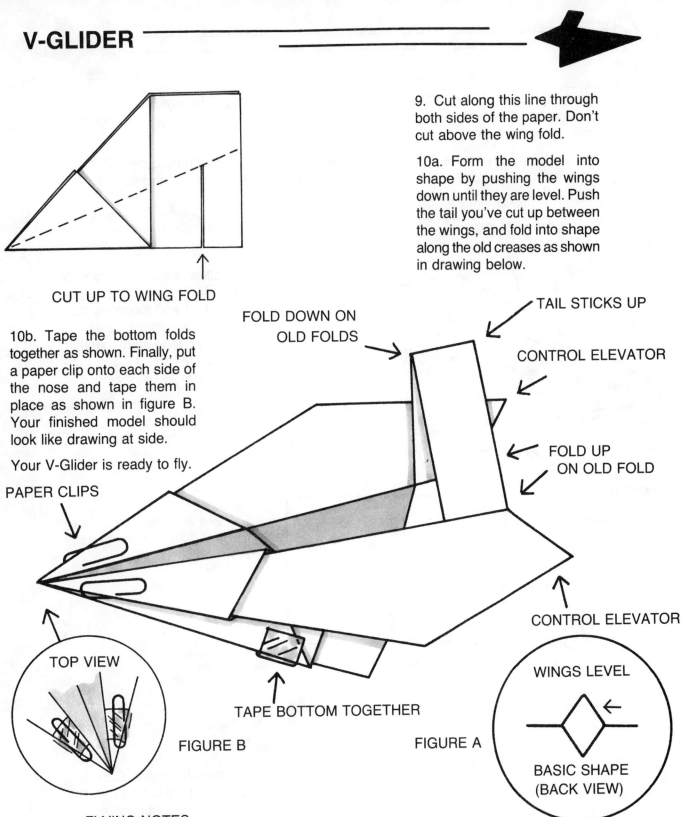

CUT UP TO WING FOLD

9. Cut along this line through both sides of the paper. Don't cut above the wing fold.

10a. Form the model into shape by pushing the wings down until they are level. Push the tail you've cut up between the wings, and fold into shape along the old creases as shown in drawing below.

TAIL STICKS UP

CONTROL ELEVATOR

FOLD DOWN ON OLD FOLDS

FOLD UP ON OLD FOLD

10b. Tape the bottom folds together as shown. Finally, put a paper clip onto each side of the nose and tape them in place as shown in figure B. Your finished model should look like drawing at side.

Your V-Glider is ready to fly.

PAPER CLIPS

CONTROL ELEVATOR

TOP VIEW

TAPE BOTTOM TOGETHER

FIGURE B

FIGURE A

WINGS LEVEL

BASIC SHAPE (BACK VIEW)

FLYING NOTES:

It's important that the tail is folded properly and doesn't lean. (See figure A.)

The two paper clips make this model's nose heavy. If you want to lengthen the glide, curve the control elevators up a little.

When you launch the V-Glider, try not to squeeze the sides together too much. The plane should be open in flight so that the tail forms an upside-down V as shown in figure A.

15

V-JET

This jet version of the V-Glider has more speed and strength. Where the V-Glider glides, the V-Jet zips, so plan to fly it outdoors. To make the V-Jet you will need two sheets of paper.

Take a piece of paper and do the Four-Step Fold. If necessary turn to page 8 for instructions. Your paper should look like step 4 of the Four-Step Fold before you continue.

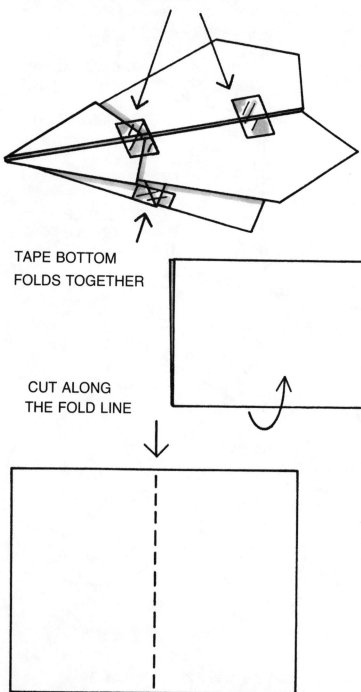

TAPE WINGS TOGETHER

TAPE BOTTOM
FOLDS TOGETHER

CUT ALONG
THE FOLD LINE

1. Follow steps 1 through 6 for the V-Glider. (Turn to pages 13 and 14 and follow instructions 1 through 7.) Level the wings and tape them together on top as shown. Also tape the bottom folds together.

2. Take another sheet of paper and fold it in half neatly the short way.

3. Open the paper. Cut carefully along the fold line so that you have two half sheets.

CONTINUED ▷   16

(½ SHEET)

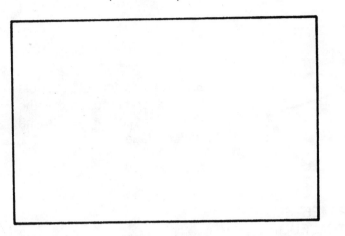

4. You will need only one half sheet to complete this model.

LINE UP SIDES

5. Fold the half sheet of paper neatly in half the long way, making sure the sides line up.

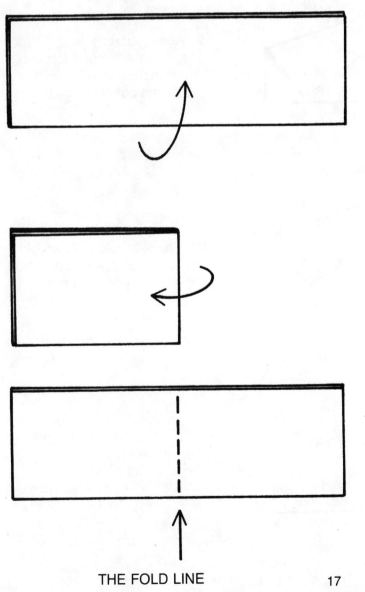

6. Now fold it in half the short way.

7. Open only the fold you just made and lay the paper flat.

THE FOLD LINE

17

CONTINUED ▷

START FOLD HERE AT THE FOLD LINE

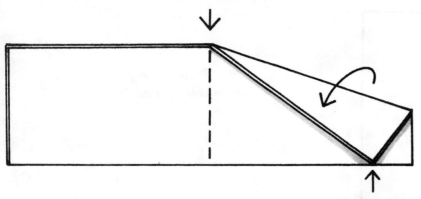

TIP MEETS
BOTTOM EDGE

8. Starting at the fold line, fold the first top corner so that the tip of the corner meets the bottom edge.

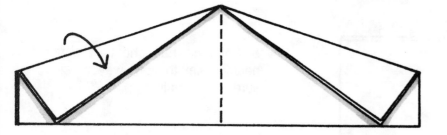

9. Again, starting at the fold line, fold the second top corner so that the tip of the corner meets the bottom edge.

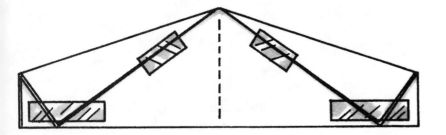

TAPE AS SHOWN

10. Press the folds firmly. Use four pieces of tape to tape the corners in place as shown.

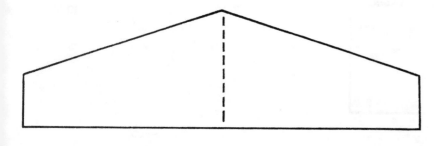

COMPLETED WING (TOP VIEW)

11. Turn your paper over, placing the taped side down. The drawing shows the top view of your completed wing.

CONTINUED ▷

LINE UP THE FOLD LINE
ON WING WITH THE
CENTER LINE OF THE
BODY. TAPE IN PLACE AS SHOWN.

TAPE
WHERE
TIPS MEET

TAPE HERE

12. Carefully place the jet's wing onto the body. Make sure that the fold line on the jet's wing is lined up with the center line of the body. Also, the center tip of the jet's wing should meet the center tip of the body. Tape the jet's wing firmly to the body as shown.

WINGS SLANT UP

FIGURE A

CONTROL
ELEVATORS

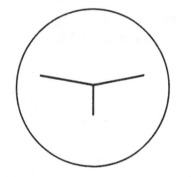

TAPE
PAPER CLIPS

BASIC SHAPE (BACK VIEW)

13. Put one paper clip on each side of the nose and tape them in place. Slant the wings up as shown in figure A. Your finished model should look like drawing above.

Your V-Jet is ready to fly.

FLYING NOTES:

This plane is really too heavy and fast for indoor flying and should be used *outdoors only*. Because the nose is heavy, you will probably have to curve up the control elevators to give the plane a long glide.

You can fly this model on a fairly breezy day by giving it a good launch upward. If after a few flights it starts to dive or spin, check to see that the wings are slanted up, the nose is straight, and the control elevators are properly fixed. With a little practice, you can fly the V-Jet high and wide!

FLYING WING

This plane's large wing gives it a smooth, slow flight.

Take a piece of paper and do the Four-Step Fold. If necessary turn to page 8 for instructions. Your paper should look like step 4 of the Four-Step Fold before you continue.

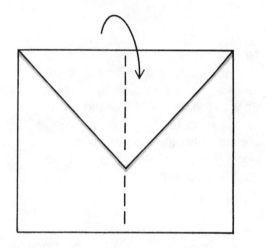

1. Fold the triangle as shown so that the tip of the triangle rests on the fold line.

2. Measure 1½ inches on both sides of the fold line.

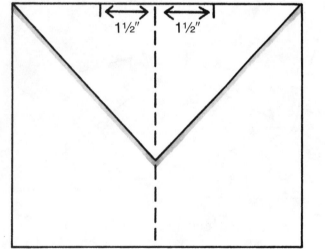

3. Starting at the right 1½-inch mark, fold the top corner so that it meets the center fold.

1½"
MARK

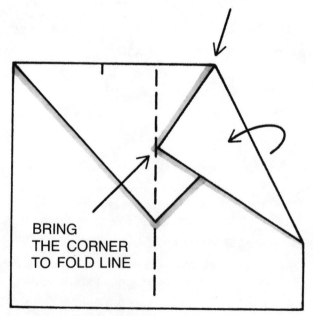

BRING
THE CORNER
TO FOLD LINE

CONTINUED ▷

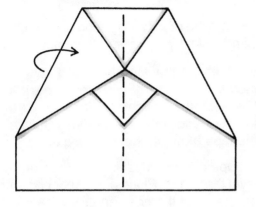

4. Starting at the left 1½-inch mark, fold the bottom corner so that it meets the other corner at the fold line.

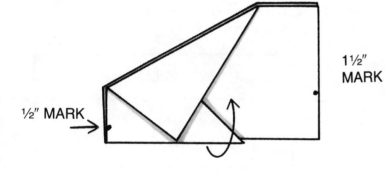

1½" MARK

½" MARK →

5. Refold the paper in half with the folds outside as shown. Use your ruler to measure 1½ inches from the bottom fold at the wide edge and make a dot. Next, measure ½ inch from the bottom fold at the narrow edge and make a dot. Use your ruler to help you draw a straight line connecting the two dots.

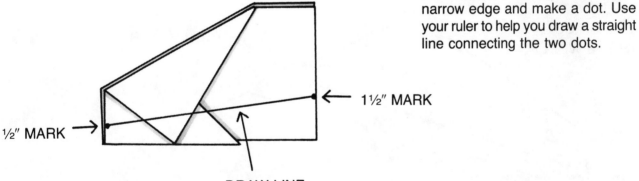

← 1½" MARK

½" MARK →

DRAW LINE

6. Keep your ruler in place beneath the line you've drawn. Using your ruler edge as a guide, fold the wing down over the ruler.

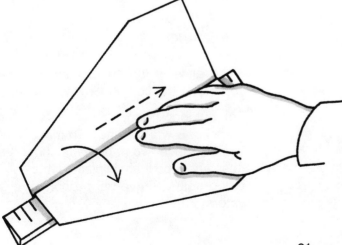

CONTINUED ▷

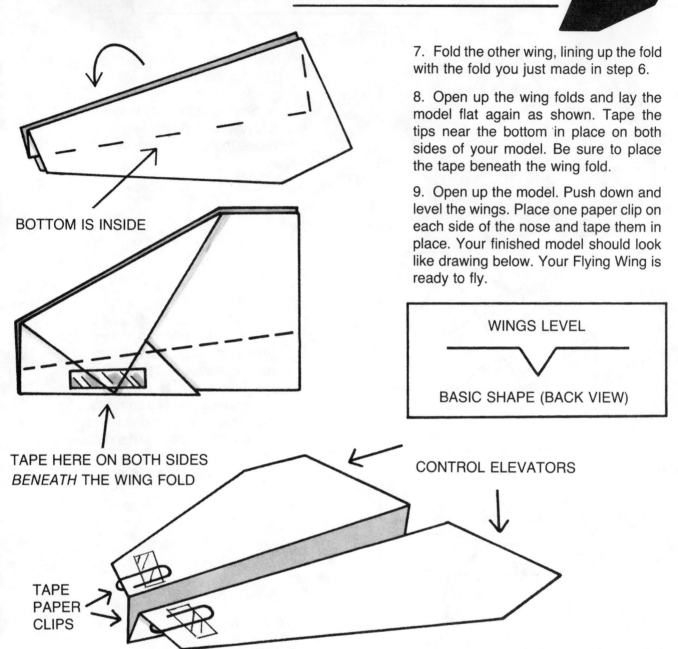

BOTTOM IS INSIDE

TAPE HERE ON BOTH SIDES
BENEATH THE WING FOLD

7. Fold the other wing, lining up the fold with the fold you just made in step 6.

8. Open up the wing folds and lay the model flat again as shown. Tape the tips near the bottom in place on both sides of your model. Be sure to place the tape beneath the wing fold.

9. Open up the model. Push down and level the wings. Place one paper clip on each side of the nose and tape them in place. Your finished model should look like drawing below. Your Flying Wing is ready to fly.

WINGS LEVEL

BASIC SHAPE (BACK VIEW)

CONTROL ELEVATORS

TAPE
PAPER
CLIPS

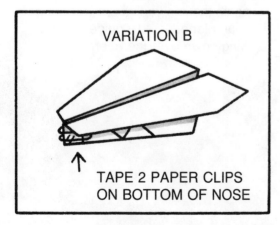

VARIATION B

TAPE 2 PAPER CLIPS
ON BOTTOM OF NOSE

FLYING NOTES:

If the glide is too short, curve up the corners of the control elevators a bit.

For outdoor flying, you may find that variation B works better. To make variation B, place two paper clips under the nose and tape them in place. If the nose is too heavy, curve up the control elevators.

HIGH WINGER

Follow the instructions carefully for this model, and you will have a great-looking plane that's ready to soar. For the best model, use 16-pound heavyweight typewriting paper or other heavyweight paper.

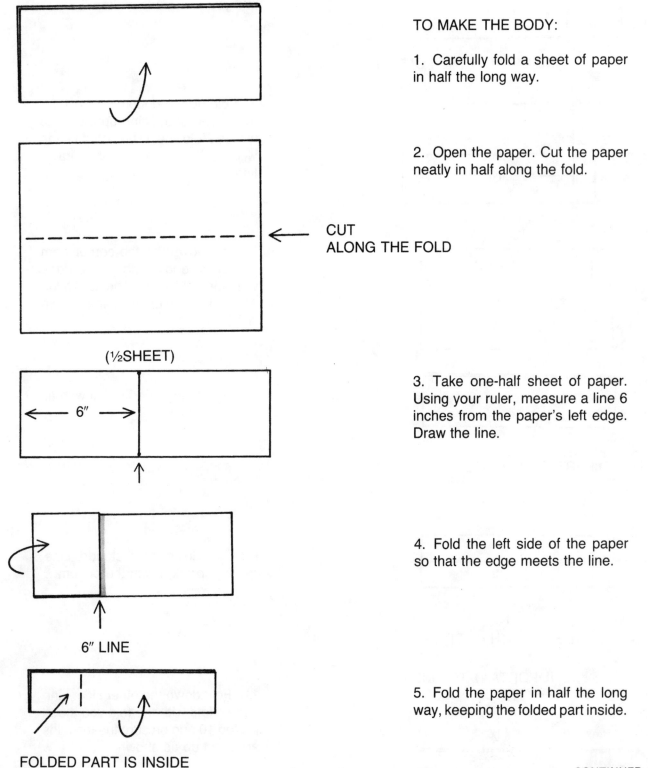

TO MAKE THE BODY:

1. Carefully fold a sheet of paper in half the long way.

2. Open the paper. Cut the paper neatly in half along the fold.

CUT
ALONG THE FOLD

(½SHEET)

3. Take one-half sheet of paper. Using your ruler, measure a line 6 inches from the paper's left edge. Draw the line.

6″

4. Fold the left side of the paper so that the edge meets the line.

6″ LINE

5. Fold the paper in half the long way, keeping the folded part inside.

FOLDED PART IS INSIDE

CONTINUED ▷

HIGH WINGER

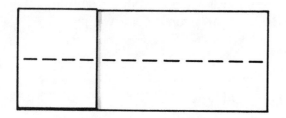

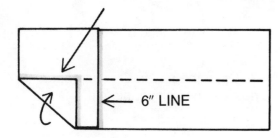

LINE UP WITH THE FOLD LINE

← 6" LINE

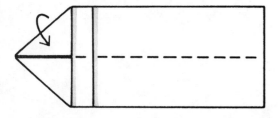

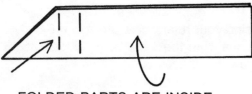

FOLDED PARTS ARE INSIDE

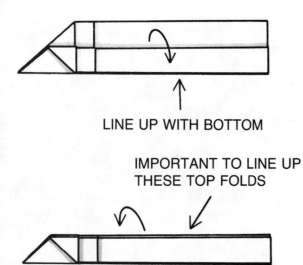

LINE UP WITH BOTTOM

IMPORTANT TO LINE UP
THESE TOP FOLDS

6. Open the paper. Undo only the fold you just made in step 5.

7. Fold up the bottom corner from the folded end, lining up the edge with the fold line. (The bottom edge will NOT line up with the drawn line.)

8. Fold down the top corner from the folded end, lining up the edge with the fold line. (The top edge will NOT line up with the drawn line.)

9. Refold the paper in half with all the folds inside.

10. Fold down the first side. Line up the top edge with the bottom.

11. Fold down the other side. Line up this fold with the fold you made in step 10 and be sure the top folds are lined up as shown.

CONTINUED ▷

HIGH WINGER

THE CREASE

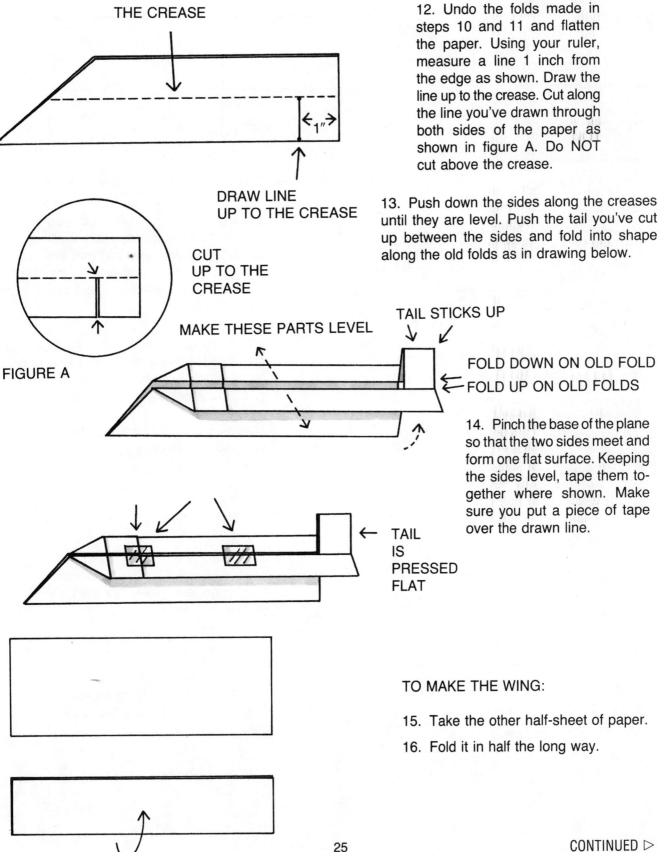

DRAW LINE
UP TO THE CREASE

CUT
UP TO THE
CREASE

FIGURE A

MAKE THESE PARTS LEVEL

TAIL STICKS UP

FOLD DOWN ON OLD FOLD

FOLD UP ON OLD FOLDS

TAIL
IS
PRESSED
FLAT

12. Undo the folds made in steps 10 and 11 and flatten the paper. Using your ruler, measure a line 1 inch from the edge as shown. Draw the line up to the crease. Cut along the line you've drawn through both sides of the paper as shown in figure A. Do NOT cut above the crease.

13. Push down the sides along the creases until they are level. Push the tail you've cut up between the sides and fold into shape along the old folds as in drawing below.

14. Pinch the base of the plane so that the two sides meet and form one flat surface. Keeping the sides level, tape them together where shown. Make sure you put a piece of tape over the drawn line.

TO MAKE THE WING:

15. Take the other half-sheet of paper.

16. Fold it in half the long way.

25

CONTINUED ▷

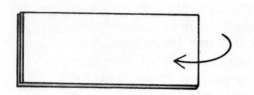

START FOLD HERE AT THE FOLD LINE

THE FOLD LINE

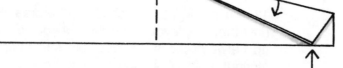

BRING TIP TO BOTTOM

17. Fold it in half the short way.

18. Open only the fold that you just made in step 17. Starting at the fold line, carefully fold one top corner (the open edge), bringing the tip of the corner to meet the bottom fold.

19. Starting at the fold line, carefully fold the other top corner (the open edge), bringing the tip of the corner to meet the bottom fold.

20. Press the folds firmly and tape as shown in drawing at left.

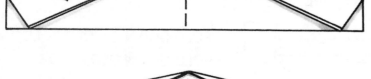

TAPE AS SHOWN

DRAW LINE   DRAW LINE

3"   3"

21. Turn the wing over. With your ruler, measure 3 inches from each wing edge, and draw two lines as shown.

3" LINE   TOP OF WING   3" LINE

22. Fold both side wing edges so that they line up with the 3-inch lines that you drew.

LINE UP
WITH WING EDGE

LINE UP
WITH WING EDGE

CONTINUED ▷

HIGH WINGER

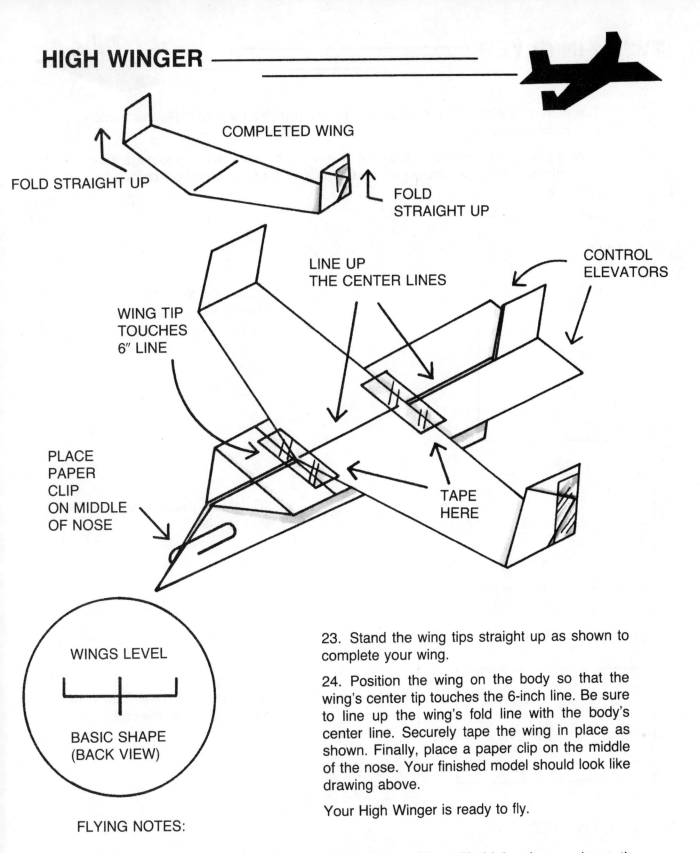

COMPLETED WING

FOLD STRAIGHT UP

FOLD STRAIGHT UP

LINE UP THE CENTER LINES

CONTROL ELEVATORS

WING TIP TOUCHES 6" LINE

PLACE PAPER CLIP ON MIDDLE OF NOSE

TAPE HERE

WINGS LEVEL

BASIC SHAPE (BACK VIEW)

23. Stand the wing tips straight up as shown to complete your wing.

24. Position the wing on the body so that the wing's center tip touches the 6-inch line. Be sure to line up the wing's fold line with the body's center line. Securely tape the wing in place as shown. Finally, place a paper clip on the middle of the nose. Your finished model should look like drawing above.

Your High Winger is ready to fly.

FLYING NOTES:

To test-fly the plane, curve up the control elevators a bit, and hold the plane underneath the front part of the wing as you launch it. If it nosedives, curve up the control elevators a little bit more. Keep doing this until the plane's flight is level. Also, make sure the nose is straight, the wings are level, and the wing tips and tail are straight up. Fly this model outdoors on a calm day.

This plane has a twin-fin in the back for a level glide. You should make this model with heavyweight paper.

Take a piece of paper and do the Four-Step Fold. If necessary turn to page 8 for instructions. Your paper should look like step 4 of the Four-Step Fold before you continue.

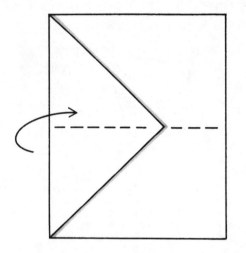

1. Carefully fold the triangle as shown so that the tip of the triangle rests on the fold line.

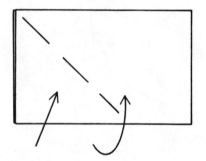

FOLDED PART IS INSIDE

2. Refold the paper in half with the folded tip inside.

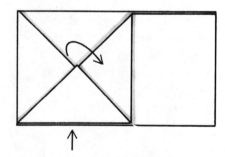

LINE UP WITH BOTTOM

3. Fold the first corner, lining up the side edge with the bottom.

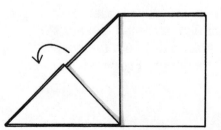

4. Fold the second corner, lining it up with the first.

CONTINUED ▷

FIGURE A

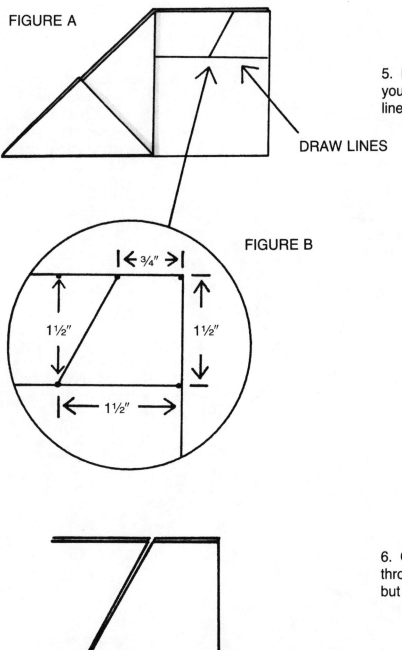

DRAW LINES

5. Following figures A and B, use your ruler to measure and draw the lines shown.

FIGURE B

USE AS A GUIDE LINE

CUT TO HERE

CLOSE-UP VIEW

6. Cut down along the slanted line through *both* sides of the paper, but do not cut past the guide line.

CONTINUED ▷

TWIN-FIN FLYER

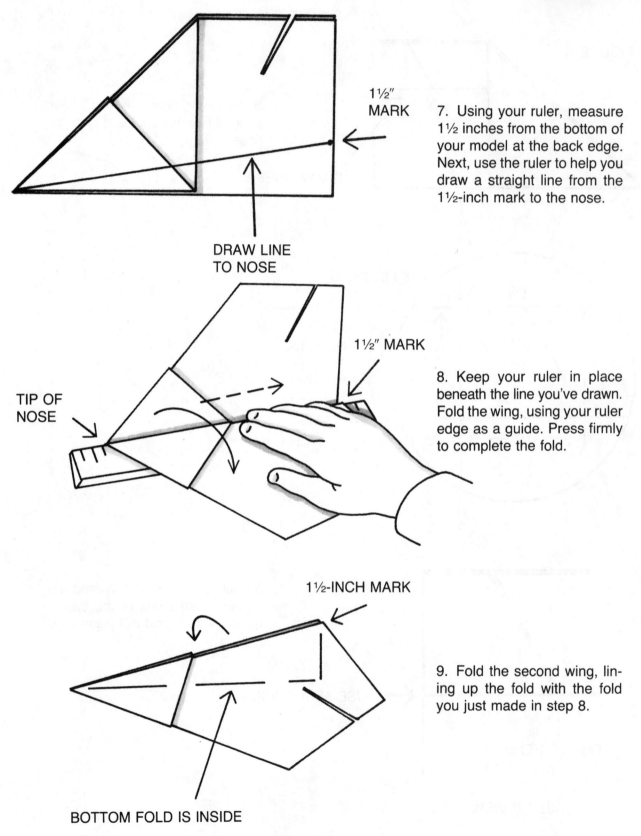

1½" MARK

7. Using your ruler, measure 1½ inches from the bottom of your model at the back edge. Next, use the ruler to help you draw a straight line from the 1½-inch mark to the nose.

DRAW LINE TO NOSE

1½" MARK

TIP OF NOSE

8. Keep your ruler in place beneath the line you've drawn. Fold the wing, using your ruler edge as a guide. Press firmly to complete the fold.

1½-INCH MARK

9. Fold the second wing, lining up the fold with the fold you just made in step 8.

BOTTOM FOLD IS INSIDE

CONTINUED ▷

TWIN-FIN FLYER

LINE UP FINS WITH EDGES OF WINGS

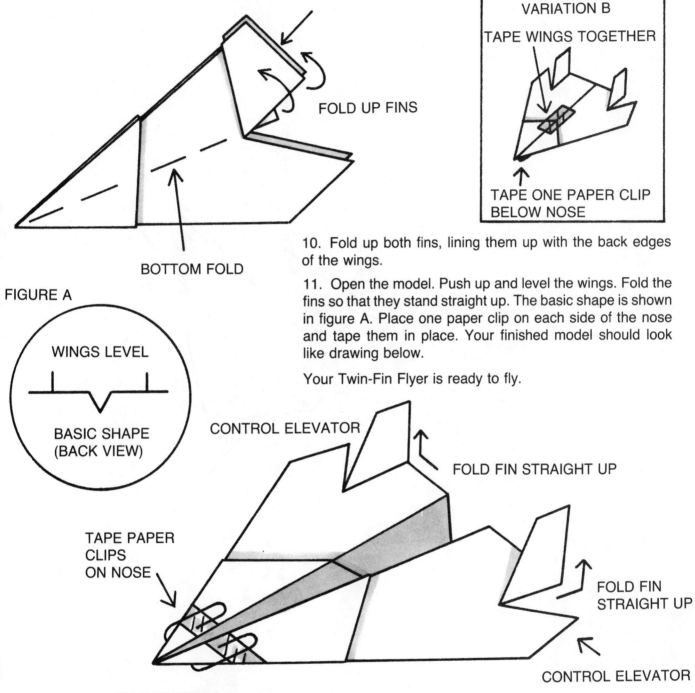

FOLD UP FINS

BOTTOM FOLD

FIGURE A

WINGS LEVEL

BASIC SHAPE
(BACK VIEW)

VARIATION B

TAPE WINGS TOGETHER

TAPE ONE PAPER CLIP
BELOW NOSE

10. Fold up both fins, lining them up with the back edges of the wings.

11. Open the model. Push up and level the wings. Fold the fins so that they stand straight up. The basic shape is shown in figure A. Place one paper clip on each side of the nose and tape them in place. Your finished model should look like drawing below.

Your Twin-Fin Flyer is ready to fly.

CONTROL ELEVATOR

FOLD FIN STRAIGHT UP

TAPE PAPER
CLIPS
ON NOSE

FOLD FIN
STRAIGHT UP

CONTROL ELEVATOR

FLYING NOTES:

If the plane nosedives or stalls, adjust the control elevators. For a smooth flight, it is very important that the fins stand straight up. (See figure above.)

If your plane doesn't fly as well as you would like or if you want a more streamlined model, try variation B. Just tape the wings together as shown. Instead of placing two paper clips on the nose, tape one paper clip below the nose.